EVOLUTION
OF
IMMORTALITY

EVOLUTION
OF
IMMORTALITY

EXTREME FUTURISM IN THE EYES OF A HUMANIST

ADAM STANCZYK

iUniverse LLC
Bloomington

EVOLUTION OF IMMORTALITY
EXTREME FUTURISM IN THE EYES OF A HUMANIST

iUniverse books may be ordered through booksellers or by contacting:

iUniverse LLC
1663 Liberty Drive
Bloomington, IN 47403
www.iuniverse.com
1-800-Authors (1-800-288-4677)

ISBN: 978-1-4917-2149-0 (sc)
ISBN: 978-1-4917-2150-6 (e)

Library of Congress Control Number: 2014902450

Printed in the United States of America.

iUniverse rev. date: 04/29/2014

In memory of my parents

CONTENTS

PREFACE

Warsaw Experience

Since the subject of techno-immortality became a hot topic of futuristic debate, I am much more optimistic about the future of humanity as well as the future of individual souls. Before revealing the basis for my optimism and the reason behind writing on such a subject, I would like to take readers to a time and place that had a profound effect on my philosophical views and on my decision to write this book.

I grew up in Warsaw, the capital of Poland, in a time when painful memories from World War II were still a subject of people's daily talks. Warsaw was one of the most devastated cities of World War II. In the beginning of 1945, after Russians forced German troops to retreat, Warsaw was a sea of ruins, mercifully covered by snow.

Most of the devastation resulted from Hitler's revenge for the city's general uprising against German occupation. This uprising came roughly fourteen months after the residents of the Jewish ghetto decided to die fighting rather than go to concentration camps. Needless to say, the uprisings failed. Moreover, in each case, Hitler ordered German troops to walk down the empty streets with explosives and flamethrowers in order to destroy any building that had withstood the relentless shelling. In both uprisings, there were tremendous civilian losses. By 1944, over 200,000 Polish citizens had died; 600,000 others escaped or were forced to leave the town, with many sent to labor or concentration camps. A small number of residents clung to life, hiding in ruins and waiting for the German occupiers to retreat.

When the town was finally liberated, all those who looked upon the ruins of Warsaw were anguished and tormented.

There was no hope for the future of the town. At the time described, Warsavians had different problems. Several times, high-ranking officials examined the whole town, together with architects and other specialists, all trying to evaluate the situation. The prevailing opinion was clear: they should leave the ruins and build a new capital elsewhere. Any attempt to rebuild the town from the ruins would be economically foolish. The nation struggled to survive the next months.

Then something strange happened, and nothing could stop it.

Before the end of the bitter-cold winter, several small groups of people began returning to the would-be town, and despite the frightful conditions, they stayed! As time went by, more and more people joined them, settling in the ruins. The silent message became clear: "We wish Warsaw to be rebuilt in its original place."

The new communist government had no choice but to agree.

This spontaneous act of the people, repeated in other Polish towns, was and is a remarkable indication of how the instincts of the nation led to the correct decision. Their hearts told them that the past and present must be bound together in a spiritual continuum. They felt that giving up the streets, the buildings, and the walls that were a part of their national identity would be a betrayal of their ancestors and, more, of themselves. These buildings, which had witnessed coronations, constitutional conventions, weddings, and wars, could not be left in a pile of rubble and ashes. They wanted to restore them at any cost.

Therefore, the nation undertook the gigantic effort to reconstruct everything to its historic originals. Today, after meticulous reconstruction of the historic center of Warsaw, this part has become a UNESCO World Heritage Site. (UNESCO is a United Nations agency responsible, among other things, for setting worldwide standards for the conservation of historical monuments.)

Being a longtime architect devoted to art, beauty, and humanist values, I applaud the decision to resurrect the town of Warsaw from the ruins. I believe that the philosophical significance of those happenings is beyond the sense of just diligent reconstruction work. I feel that being so close to the Polish drama of survival made me see those happenings as being transcendental.

The Warsaw experience reveals a story of strong emotional bonds with the past. Many years later, we are in desperate need to create the same bonds between the present and the *future*. Seeing some of today's problems, it is obvious to me that humanity's collective and individual fate will depend on the strength of those bonds. That is why I decided to write this book.

Is the subject of immortality suitable for an architect?

Within the last several decades, the ideas of immortality have become an increased interest of scientists and technologists. As a result, several concepts of immortality within the natural law were produced. Some concepts went as far as to propose a physical mechanism to revive the dead and arrange a future perfect world (more about those concepts further in this book).

I believe that almost all of those ideas may become, to some degree, inspirational, forcing certain people to think differently about the future of our planet. However, what I would like to see in those ideas is a more humanistic orientation, allowing us to understand and feel the presented concepts without being lost in technical issues. Therefore, I decided to join the immortality debate, believing that as an architect and humanist, I can offer valuable observations and suggestions to make the idea of immortality more believable to the average person.

Immortality is more or less a futuristic idea. Any futurism requires knowledge about a large variety of issues. I hope that my multidisciplinary knowledge (required to be a successful architect) is suitable for the task.

ACKNOWLEDGMENTS

My special thanks to my wife, for her patience and encouragement while I worked on this book.

My special gratitude to Bonnie and Don Torgerson and Elaine and Johan Willers for being such great friends and mentors during our family's emigration.

My appreciation for my good friends and scientists Alicja and Jacek Bielawski (chemistry), Hanna Gracz, Ludwik Sujkowski (physics), and Stephanie Hurt (organization behavior, HR, and international strategies) for sharing with me their professional opinions about some of the issues of my book.

My appreciation for Julia Żylina-Chudzik for permission to use her elaboration on philosophy of Common Cause, written by nineteenth-century philosopher Nikolai Fyodorov.

My appreciation for my good friends and neighbors Jamie Jones, Kim Massey and Wade Rowlings, for their assistance with some English expressions.

Finally, my appreciation for the iUniverse editorial staff for making my manuscript such a nice piece of prose.

INTRODUCTION

Revival of the longtime dead within the natural law seems like pure fantasy. Yet some renowned thinkers contemplate such happening as a rational future possibility. Of course, there are other scaled-down ideas of immortality. Unfortunately, they could benefit only those who are lucky to be alive in a certain time and place.

No matter what anybody may think about the revival of the dead, it is the only concept that I see as able to meet humanist principles. In addition, such an idea might have the best chance to motivate today's society to do more to make our planet habitable for the future generations.

Can immortality through revival of the dead prove to be credible, or should we concentrate just on the scaled-down version of immortality?

This book will take readers into a hot debate about the immortality ideas and their possible impact on the present and future societies.

This book is written for open-minded individuals, as it involves some far-reaching expectations, stretching beyond everyday thoughts. In the core of those expectations is the notion that humans have a much higher capacity than many are willing to give credit for. Some people, including the author of this book, believe that mankind has an astonishing capacity to cultivate our destiny.

The idea of immortality presented in this book involves a tremendous number of issues, and I am aware that they are not all resolved. Nevertheless, I did my best to address those issues I consider to be the most critical. The book is divided into two parts. The first part presents and compares two main ideas of immortality proposed in the last decades by some scientists and technologists. This part contains my conclusion about which idea should be promoted to guide humanity's future and why. The first part ends with a declaration of this book's philosophical neutrality.

The second part of the book presents some additional factors supporting the promoted idea, together with my response to typical criticism about similar ideas in the past.

In the last chapter, readers will find a summary of the most critical arguments presented throughout this book.

Since this book mentions humanist principles and refers to the transhumanist movement, I decided to display the official Humanist and Transhumanist Declarations in appendix 1 and appendix 2.

PART 1

CHAPTER I

Ideas and Motivations

Two dreams came down to earth one night
From the realm of mist and dew;
One was the dream of the old, old days,
And one was a dream of the new.
—Eugene Field

*T*he truth is that nobody can predict, for certain, the ultimate fate of our life; nobody can even guarantee our collective survival over the next century. However, I believe that we can greatly improve our odds. I have been thinking about the growing debate over the idea of immortality, claimed by some to be achievable through advanced science and technology.

Is such a thing realistic? When? In what form? What negatives or positives may techno-immortality offer now and in the future?

Judging by the scale of the required human achievement and the scale of psychological impact, I distinguished two general ideas of immortality, which I am going to discuss. The better known idea of immortality claims as follows:

With advanced science and technology, humanity will stop aging and make all diseases curable.

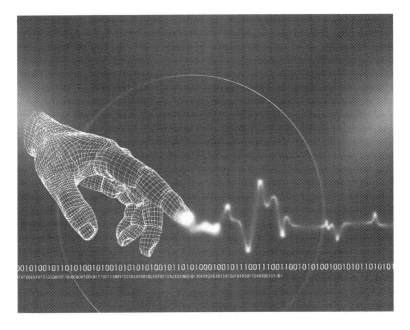

This idea, known as **biological immortality**, proclaims immunity from death caused by aging or terminal disease. Among the names associated with this idea I would list Aubrey de Grey, a researcher who has developed a series of biomedical rejuvenation strategies to reverse human aging, and Raymond Kurzweil, a renowned technologist, futurist, and inventor. Recently, Kurzweil invigorated the immortality debate by predicting that the biological immortality era will start by the year 2045 (*The Singularity Is Near*). In this book and some previous publications, Kurzweil points at the rapid evolutionary transformation of our species. He claims that we are about to reach a critical time of technological development, known as a singularity. Technological singularity is considered by some to be the theoretical point in time when artificial intelligence exceeds human intelligence. Interestingly enough, Kurzweil has been known to make very accurate predictions in the past. One of them was his prediction of the dramatic expansion in worldwide Internet use by the year 2000. He made this prediction when the Internet was in its early stage and used by only a fraction of the people who go online today.

What do I think about the subject idea?

Unfortunately, the described immortality (with the adjective "biological") will not prevent people from dying in traumatic events, such as accidents, wars, or criminal acts. I have a lot of respect for the authors of the concept of biological immortality. However, from a humanist perspective, I see substantial limitations in the idea. Such an idea would benefit only a part of humanity, those lucky to live in a certain place and time. Many just may not have what it will take to become biologically immortal. The notion that only some will be in the right place and thus have access to therapies may become a big ethical and political problem in the decades or centuries to come.

Other concerns about the biological immortality era are outlined in chapter VIII of this book.

The second idea of immortality may be seen as a bold extension of the idea of biological immortality. This idea claims as follows:

In a long run of evolution, humanity will develop the ability to revive the dead and achieve total immortality.

Please do not look in this book for any indication of what entity (God? Nature?) could empower humanity to do such an extraordinary task. Chapter VI explains my position on those philosophical questions.

Whatever one may think about the **total immortality** idea, it seems to offer full compliance with humanist principles. It is fair and inclusive in treatment of human beings. It is not limited to a certain time and space. The ability to revive the longtime dead, if real, would open fantastic possibilities for creating immortality, with perfect justice for all, working even retroactively.

Should serious rational people consider such a possibility?

My answer is yes! The idea shows surprising strength when specific questions confront it. In other words, it is much easier to criticize (or ridicule) the entire idea in general terms than issue by issue. Therefore, I invite readers to play with the subject claim a little bit longer before deciding to quit.

From my perspective, I see three critical issues, which the idea of total immortality (immortality via revival of the dead) must resolve to work, at least in principle. The issues/questions seem to be as follows:

Ability: What is the basis to expect that humankind would ever have the extraordinary *ability* to revive the longtime dead?

Desire: The science of evolution teaches us that the chain of evolution leads back to increasingly less intelligent species. Is it rational to expect that our mighty descendants may have a *desire* to take on the burden of reviving strange and primitive creatures from the past? An additional question is, at which point of the evolutionary chain is the process of revival supposed to stop? Are we going to revive the bugs?

Sense: Let's assume for a moment that our descendants have the *ability* and *desire* to revive the past generations and that people can live forever. Can eternal life have *sense* (meaning) when anything could be postponed indefinitely without losing a day? What may be the driving force for any activity beyond the necessity to survive? What would prevent society from becoming a mental colony of microbes?

Those three issues are often raised during the immortality debate and are considered impossible to resolve within natural law. Also, I have to admit that my first thought about the issues of desire and sense was that there is no way anybody could find positive and rational answers for them.

However, I was wrong. Quite logical and positive answers exist, and I offer them in chapters II through IV of this book. Before we go to the next chapters, here is a little historical background about the subject:

The idea of the human ability to revive the longtime dead first surfaced in the work of Russian philosopher-futurist Nikolai Fyodorov (1829–1903). Due to the specific time of Fyodorov's life, his publications became known only after his death. Nevertheless, one may admire this philosopher's vision of such an extraordinary development in human ability when many later discoveries and marvels of modern technology were still unknown. As a reminder, Fyodorov died at the time of the Wright Brothers' first flight: December 17, 1903.

Living in the nineteenth century, Fyodorov could not support his idea of total immortality by any technical specifics. Instead, he touched many important issues of methodology and ethics. Chapter V is entirely designated to his philosophy, which he called the Common Cause.

At the end of the last century, the idea of immortality via revival of the dead was promoted by some renowned thinkers, such as Frank Tipler and Hans Moravec (I am sure that the list is longer). In 1994, Tipler, an American cosmologist and expert in mathematics, physics, and computation, published *The Physics of Immortality: Modern Cosmology, God and the Resurrection of the Dead*. In this book, he claims that general resurrection will be possible in the future through an all-knowing mega-computer. Such a computer, he claimed, would be constructed far in the future by an extremely advanced civilization. Moravec, an Austrian futurist and expert in robotics and artificial intelligence, also envisioned a computer system playing a critical role in the resurrection of life (see his numerous publications, including the 1990 book *Mind Children*).

Nikolai Fyodorov and the more recent authors (Tipler, Moravec, de Grey, and Kurzweil) are representatives of an international philosophy known as transhumanism. The goal of this movement is to lift human capacities to the highest possible level, through advanced science and technology. Of course, immortality and revival of the dead so far belong to the most ambitious goals.

I owe an apology to all four authors of the modern era for the extremely short characterization of their interesting publications on the subject of immortality. However, my role is not to look for a specific technical solution to reach some immortality objectives. If we are lucky to survive as long, we will have millions (or billions) of years to uncover the secrets of life and death and find the right way to reach the unthinkable. We can always rely on the undisputed effects of time and evolution as an indication that such a future will be possible.

Therefore, we can wait for the right scientific solution for how to revive the dead. What we cannot do is wait (sit tight) and let humanity become extinct while doing nothing to improve the odds of our survival.

My role as a humanist is to promote ideas that are rational and motivating and that work with quite complicated human nature. I believe that the idea of total immortality through revival of the dead matches the required conditions. For a long time, I struggled to find logical and positive answers to the questions of our descendants' *desire* to revive the past generations and *sense* of eternal life. Once I had those answers, I saw the entire idea of immortality as quite natural and realistic. I hope that readers will feel the same after reading through this book.

I want to repeat how important it is to change society's lethargic attitude toward the future of our planet.

Everybody knows that motivating ideas and goals that aim high add "wings." In my career as an architect, I witnessed this phenomenon almost every day, working with a number of people in different environments and in more than one country.

People engaged in ambitious, highly complex projects generate more dedication and a better work ethic than do those working on smaller, less significant jobs. This simply proves that motivation (or the lack thereof) plays a quite substantial role in whether or not human endeavor is effective. The call to conquer death and revive the past generations is just that. This idea seems to be the best candidate to awaken society to an appropriate action. It has the potential to induce people to do for the future of our planet what scientists and environmentalists have been seeking for decades.

I see immortality through the revival of the dead as a game changer. Suddenly, problems like our planet's deteriorating environment, threats of nuclear war, or lack of preparation to meet cosmic challenges may become very important. Simply, many may start thinking about the possible connection between their fate and the fate of our descendants.

Everybody knows what action needs to be taken. We must immediately halt environmental degradation and start working on technologies to meet the challenges to humanity's continued existence.

In all of the urgency to act, the right idea about immortality must be chosen, including a thorough analysis of its problems and benefits to society. However, we should never abandon the quest for immortality because some vocal opponents feel it is just a fantasy or point at artificial problems. As I describe further in this book, there is too much at stake.

The next several decades will be critical to our chances to survive. Let's be optimistic. Let's believe that in our human capacity is much more than just an opportunity to buy newer cars or TV sets.

CHAPTER II

Ability

The only way of finding the limits of the possible is by going beyond them into the impossible.

　　　　　　　—Arthur C. Clarke

C an future human generations or alien civilizations develop technologies to resurrect the dead? In this chapter, we will explore the issue of *ability*. I italicized this word to underline that nothing else will be discussed in this chapter (other issues and questions are addressed in other chapters).

Of course, the expectation of this ability is extraordinary and may raise some doubts. However, we have to remember that we are judging an ability of future entities (our descendants) being a million times smarter than we are. Considering the age of our planet, humanity seems to be at the dawn of development. Therefore, here is the simple logic behind the idea that it is possible to revive the dead:

The theory of evolution is recognized by most scientists as one of the best-documented pieces of scientific work. One hundred fifty years of scientific findings and extensive testing provided so much evidence that even the Vatican recognized that evolution was the real way life was created. In a 1996 message to the Pontifical Academy of Sciences, Pope John Paul II called evolution "an essential subject which deeply interests the Church."

One of the extraordinary things brought up by science is the finding that a human ancestor was nothing more than a one-cell microbe living on our planet 3.5 billion years ago. The following images of humanity's amazing transformation depict what happened next to the present time.

Beginning of all life　　　　　　　*Early human*

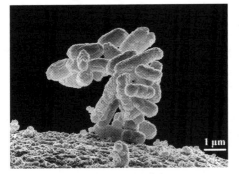 

A magnified closter of E. coli bacteria and reconstruction of Homo heidelbergensis (author: Jose Luis Martinez Alvarez);

Today

*The Space Shuttle Atlantis atop the Shuttle
Carrier Aircraft (photo: Carla Thomas, NASA).
Source of all images; Wikipedia Commons.*

Any consistent thinker who *truly* accepts that such change took place must also accept the possibility of the same (or greater) human transformation in the future.

We know very well that there is no numerical value that could possibly reflect the difference between the colony of microbes and modern human society. Therefore, regarding the abilities of humans in the future, we should not accept any limitations as long as tasks do not contain logical contradictions (an example of this contradiction is the famous question whether God could create a stone so heavy that he could not lift it).

Those who point at the incredible complexity of the human body and claim that our soul disappears at our death do not amuse me at all. We gained the ability to serve millions of mobile phone calls each day without interference of the sound waves. Why would retrieving a human soul be impossible? Skepticism or denials must also be consistent. Those who insist that a phenomenon of consciousness will be in the full grip of science cannot deny the ability of future science to retrieve a man's soul. Either everything is reducible to physical data or there are some irreducible inner tangibles out of anybody's reach.

I cannot treat today's skepticism about the range of our future abilities as anything more than a lack of imagination. Sometimes skepticism is necessary to prevent disasters like the 1912 sinking of the *Titanic* or the 1934 *Hindenburg* airship disaster. We know that in those cases, design mistakes and safety negligence led to the disasters. However, we do not want skepticism to be an automatic reaction to something extraordinary because, for instance, it is "too good to be true."

So far, in the prediction of future achievements, objectionists revealed only bad judgment and lack of imagination. It is really fun to look at the long list of predictions that went wrong.

Humankind's control over nature is a function of time; therefore, setting limitations on the future human ability without proposing any time frame is just senseless. We can only smile at the following image depicting the universe seen just about six hundred years ago. We should consider that no more than six hundred years from now, the claims of human limitations would be of no better value.

A history of incredible successes in breaking secrets like the Mayan language, espionage codes, and criminal cases indicates that there are many ways to retrieve data from tiny pieces of material information.

Although manual excavations remain the preferred method, today's archaeologists use increasingly more advanced technology in uncovering the past. Using ground-penetrating radar, archaeologists can detect the outline of buildings beneath the ground without using a shovel. Computers are then able to reconstruct an archaeological site and create a model of hidden underground structures.

We have made successful inferences about our past from scraps of old documents, pottery, and mummified bodies. Armed with sophisticated instruments like x-rays and CT scans, we are able to reconstruct bone structures of longtime-deceased people to near-perfection. Scientists invented a microscope powerful enough to view atoms so that researchers can build molecules and nanomachines. Let's keep in mind that in front of us there are millions (or perhaps billions) of years to improve our ability to uncover the past. However, I do not think that we will need as much time to reach the *ability* to revive the dead. Please keep in mind that this *ability* will be the subject of constant growth, as described in chapter IV.

Anthropologists are divided about whether human evolution has slowed down or is faster than ever before. However, the progress in science and technology is very visible, and many believe that it is growing exponentially.

What does the term *exponentially* mean? It is depicted by a legend about a mighty ruler who agreed to give a poor man a number of rice grains calculated as the exponential growth of the grains from the first square of a chessboard through the sixty-fourth.

Such a pattern requires doubling the number in each square to come to the final number at the sixty-fourth square. Here is the sum of all grains on all sixty-four squares:

One grain in the first square + 2 grains in the second square + 4 + 8 ... and so on, for the total of 18,446,744,073,709,551,615 (over 18 million, million, million grains) on the last square. This would cover the entire planet with a layer of rice grains. This is a much higher number than most people intuitively would expect.

This should be a reminder to all skeptics to not fall into a trap of making the wrong prediction of an outcome involving possible exponential growth.

The miracle of evolution together with the likelihood of exponential growth favors bold predictions about the ability of future civilizations. Please keep in mind that up to now, nothing else was discussed but the question of *ability*. The two other critical questions, *desire* and *sense*, are addressed in the next chapters.

Being revived to another life is one of many extraordinary human dreams. I do not know of any of the dreams that do not become part of our daily routine. Not so long ago, all of the following dreams were considered pure fantasy:

The dream to move exceptionally fast. I do not think that I need to list all the machines that now make this possible: racecars, speedboats, supersonic planes, and space shuttles.

The dream to see somebody far away in a crystal ball. Of course, this has been made possible thanks to television and computer screens. This dream has actually been exceeded, as the distance of visual communication is now some hundreds of millions of miles away.

The dream to see through solid objects. Incredible, but with special instruments, we can now see through solid walls or layers of the soil via radar or x-ray technology.

The dream to become invisible. Numerous publications indicate that production of special invisibility cloaks is just around the corner.

Recently, we read the shocking news that some instruments can read people's minds, word by word. Let's hope that this ability will never be used against humanist principles.

CHAPTER III

Desire

Why do I think it is rational to expect that our descendants should have any *desire* to revive endless crowds of past generations? Moreover, the subsequent question is, where should the process of revival stop, understanding that the evolutionary chain leads to less and less intelligent species?

Here are the answers:

We should not worry too much about adaptation of humans revived from different eras to the superior civilization of the future. The ability to revive our ancestors may be reached fast enough that there would not be a very dramatic change in humanity's appearance or intelligence. How much evolutionary change should one expect, we do not know. Opinions on the speed of evolution cover a broad range, from that of "evolution doesn't exist" to that of "humans will continue to evolve." There is also an opinion that technological progress will accelerate; however, the traditional biological evolution may lose its dynamics. The point was made that most of humanity lives in a more comfortable and uniform environment, making the jungle rule, "the fittest survive," almost obsolete.

Future genetic engineering is expected to help ease the differences in mental capacity between generations living in different historical eras. In general, a civilization able to revive the longtime dead should find a way to help past generations gradually join the culture and intelligence level of the future society.

With no special circumstances against revival of past generations, the *desire* of our descendants should be guaranteed by the following four factors:

- **social bonds**
- **need for justice**
- **scientific curiosity**
- **higher civility and compassion**

Author's grandparents and mother

1. <u>Social bonds</u>. Social bonds are commonly visible among families, friends, or people we love, admire, or feel gratitude toward for something they have done for us. Nikolai Fyodorov saw our descendants' *desire* to revive their ancestors as a result of strong blood bonds between generations and the descendants' moral obligation to bring their ancestors to life.

This expectation is based on the observation that in normal circumstances, most of us would like our families and friends to be around forever.

Many will agree that we expect the same *desire* from our descendants.

As Fyodorov believed, the revival may be done successively in the ancestral line: sons and daughters of the descendants restore their fathers and mothers, and they in turn revive their parents' sisters and brothers, and the cycle continues.

In case of a bloodline being broken because somebody died with no offspring, Fyodorov pointed at the general human obligation to not concede that our ancestors, who gave us life and culture, are left to die. In other words, the revival may be sponsored by friends or just the rule of the future society. However, Fyodorov seemed to stop short of explaining what the eternal society is supposed to do with parents who murder their children or vice versa. He also did not indicate what our mighty descendants should do with some real human monsters from the past.

I believe that chapter XI offers quite rational answers to those and other important questions of life in eternity.

Fyodorov seemed to concentrate exclusively on the *social bonds* as a factor strong enough to literally force our descendants to bring to life the past generations. However, in my own opinion, there are other factors that should make our descendants revive the longtime dead. Here they are:

2. <u>Need for justice</u>. Luckily, this is encoded in many of us. It is rational to expect that our descendants will have a rather higher need for justice than the present worldwide society.

In the future eternal world, there will be a pressure to revisit some cases where the deceased person was a victim of a wrong court decision. I cannot imagine that society having an ability to bring someone to life would let misjudged cases remain untouched just because a person was buried. Therefore, the legal system will most likely include the resolution of past unresolved or questionable cases. Perhaps all trials will be revisited, just in case of a jury's possible mistake. By the way, these retrials may be quite entertaining spectacles for the eternal society.

3. <u>Scientific curiosity</u>. This is the main engine driving discoveries. Just as scientists study human archaeology, future science will also study the lives of past generations. Scientists today seek grants to resurrect a dinosaur or even a Neanderthal to study.

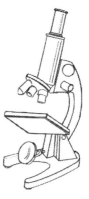

It is possible that all efforts to uncover the past are driven by a subconscious feeling of unity among the past, present, and future. Such a feeling seems to be written in human nature, and it is only natural to expect that scientists will continue pushing for examination of living representatives of past generations from different eras.

Misery of beggars drawn by Jacques Callot

4. <u>Higher civility and compassion</u>. It is also rational to expect in the future a higher level of civility and compassion. I believe that society today has substantially more civility and compassion than in the past. Those who have doubts should think about the past crowds of beggars, state-sanctioned slavery, cruelty, and all kinds of atrocities and admit that we are a better society now than ever.

Although there are still many acts of barbaric behavior, any such act usually finds worldwide outrage and condemnation. Countries often overturn oppressive regimes in an attempt to establish democratic rule. Today, there are more democratic governments than ever. All of these facts justify optimism that the level of compassion will be an additional factor reinforcing our descendants' desire to revive the dead (readers may find more justification on this claim in chapter XI).

All together, these four factors demonstrate that future generations should logically have unquestionable *desire* to bring back to life all their ancestors. However, the issue of "all their ancestors" raises one important question:

At which point of human evolution should the revival of the dead stop? If we trust the science of evolution, the ancestral line of all species leads back to increasingly more primitive forms of life. Are we going to resurrect microbes?

The answer to this question came to me a couple of years ago, while I was watching a National Geographic program on TV about dinosaurs. One episode showed an animation of a long column of Camarasauruses, huge grass-eating animals, being followed by a pack of T. rex dinosaurs. As we know, T. rex is considered to be the most terrifying carnivore to ever walk on Earth. In the TV show, these ferocious predators picked juvenile Camarasauruses from the pack and devoured them. Interestingly, no adult Camarasaurus attempted to defend its offspring. The narrator commented that the dinosaurs were too primitive to develop social bonds.

Here we go. The blood or social bonds weaken proportionally to the intelligence of the species. At some point, perhaps at the dawn of humanity, the bonds should cease to exist, together with the demand to renew such species.

Some questions may remain about the "point of no return"; however, I am sure that all of them are resolvable.

This concludes my answer to the question of *desire*, the second critical condition necessary to make immortality through revival of the dead a workable idea.

CHAPTER IV

Sense

C an eternal life have sense? Quite often, critics of eternal life imagined such a state as meaningless, boring, and not worthy of getting into. The statement that eternal life is "not desirable" is not rare.

Here is a quote from science-fiction writer Isaac Asimov (1920–1992): "There is nothing frightening about an eternal dreamless sleep. Surely it is better than eternal torment in Hell and eternal boredom in Heaven."

First, I want to respond to the comparison of eternal death to an "eternal dreamless sleep." Calling death "an eternal dreamless sleep" is too much of a spin. There is a big difference between eternal death and normal sleep, whether the sleep is dreamless or full of dreams. Sleep is part of our life's daily routine. We wake up, usually refreshed and ready for new activities. Death often comes as a scary and painful ordeal. Even if it comes in a rare gentle form, it makes us irrelevant and often hard to deal with by the surviving family and friends.

Second, it is true that boredom is a poor motivator, as it leads to lethargy and degradation of the intellect. But why in the world do some people automatically assume that eternal life must be meaningless and boring? In this book, I am going to demonstrate that one should expect the opposite. I cannot speak for religious versions of an afterlife, but the sort of eternal life arranged by a highly intelligent society should be full of meaningful and exciting activities.

To explain the driving factor for such activities, we need to envision the most natural future developments step-by-step. I emphasized the performance of evolution, and now we only need to combine the evolution factor with what we know about the average person's needs and dreams.

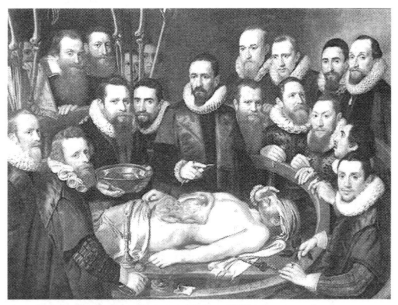

Anatomy lesson of Dr. Willem van der Meer by Michiel Jansz van Mierevelt

Step 1. Based on many futurists' opinions, it is rational to expect that life longevity and techno-immortality ideas will be a growing interest of all generations. The immediate benefit from these ideas will be that society would increase its interest to improve the conditions on which humanity's survival depends. Successes with extending life span and advanced technologies must lead to increased ability to "repair" and reanimate a body who has been damaged in traumatic events. It is only a matter of time before resuscitation techniques will lift the barriers of life.

Step 2. I agree with futurists like Aubrey de Grey and Raymond Kurzweil who say that the secrets of the human body will be known to science well enough to stop the process of aging and cure all diseases. How soon will it happen? No one can be certain; however, we can hope that a good pace of progress in the ability to repair and resuscitate a damaged body will follow quickly.

Step 3. A significant aspect of the history of human control over nature is that such progress has been gradual and unremarkable. Within the last two hundred years, the life span has more than doubled without anyone paying attention to it. People are even reluctant to recognize such an achievement, pointing at statistical gimmicks, previous vulnerability of children dying at birth, and so on. Therefore, we may expect that the future life span will extend to many thousands of years without anybody's wondering about that. All related improvements will most likely be very gradual and widespread in research labs, emergency-room procedures, genetics, biological engineering, regenerative medicine, and microbiology. Today, we are already aware of nanotechnology, which is expected to produce many medical nanorobots. Some robots will be designed to enter our bloodstream and repair interior organs. We already expect that nanotechnology will be a breakthrough in the human ability to save lives.

Step 4. At the beginning, bringing a human back to life may only be possible shortly after their death. Over time, the increased technology will make the question of how long somebody has been dead less relevant. The threshold in the ability to revive the dead will be raised over and over again and become the norm in people's minds.

Step 5. Medical knowledge and technology will not always be advanced enough to revive human remains having a high level of disintegration. Some of the cases will require the deceased to wait in graves until appropriate knowledge and technology is developed. In a typical case, all living will meet traumatic death many times, each time being brought to life again and again.

In conclusion, the true immortality of life will consist of life-death-revival parts in cyclical mode.

It seems that nobody else has discussed openly the necessity of the life-death-revival cycles as an unavoidable pattern of real immortality. To me it is obvious. As long as we are humans, we will make errors, and some of the errors will lead to somebody's death. The only way to make life really immortal is through a constantly growing ability to revive the dead.

The life-death-revival cycles of immortality should not be confused with the idea of reincarnation. In reincarnation, the essence of being human disappears in one of many animal forms. In the idea presented in this book, each immortality cycle brings humans to increasingly higher levels of complexity and sophistication.

Reincarnation and the idea of universal immortality are just two different things.

Since there are endless possibilities of encountering traumatic death, the life-death-revival cycles will most likely continue as long as humanity exists. In such a case, today's traditional expression "ashes to ashes" at the end of a future funeral ceremony may change to "life to life."

It is logical to expect that the proportion between the three elements of the immortality cycle will change over time. Let's keep in mind that human progress will never stop. The uninterrupted life span will be constantly increasing, and the time of being dead and waiting for revival will be decreasing, and one may expect that the revival from death will be increasingly easy and quick. The closest example of such cycles is the sinuisoidal line depicting the growing amplitude of life (the dashed line in the following graph).

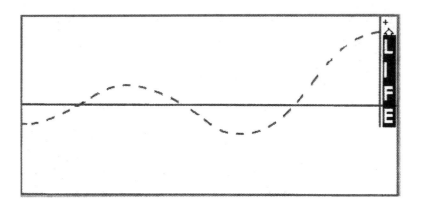

The constant progress in the conquest of death should make the life-death-revival cycles a quite attractive form of immortality. The continuous (uninterrupted) existence in permanent bliss promised by some religions may seem to offer a more attractive afterlife, but without a total change of our nature and identity, it is hardly realistic.

The most important role of the life-death-revival cycles is that even a remote possibility of a traumatic death sometimes, somewhere, makes the time factor valuable. Therefore, the entire eternal life (through the cycles) will maintain its *sense*. Like today, our descendants will always stay busy lifting their knowledge and technology to higher levels to improve the odds of survival.

As we know, humanity faces many life-threatening challenges. Most future challenges will likely come from the cosmos. According to astronomers' observations, the universe is a very turbulent place. The challenges of exploding stars, massive black holes, and many other cosmic events should keep the immortal civilization busy developing technologies to overcome these threats. Time will always be valuable because survival of some cosmic events will require extraordinary technical abilities and extensive preparation.

There is really no reason to be concerned about the prospect of "boredom" in heaven. The *sense* of eternal life can be preserved, and such life can be full of peace, harmony, creativity, and happiness.

Is this, the future awaiting all human beings, good and bad? I do not think so. The future immortal life should offer the most justice ever. Chapter XI presents more on the issue of future justice.

This concludes my argument that all three conditions of the idea of immortality and revival of the dead—*ability*, *desire,* and *sense*—have some good answers. I am aware that there may be more questions about the subject of immortality; however, no other question seems to be as critical as those just presented.

CHAPTER V

Philosophy of the Common Cause

A s I already mentioned, society owes appreciation to the three pioneers proclaiming the idea of immortality and revival of the dead: Nikolai Fyodorov, Hans Moravec, and Frank Tipler. One can especially admire Fyodorov's courage because he lived not long after the last man was executed by the infamous Spanish Inquisition.

Nikolai Fyodorov was born in 1829, just three years after the inquisition tribunal hanged Cayetano Ripoll, who was accused of heresy for teaching deism to his students. (Deism is a belief in God's existence but holds that God does not intervene with the functioning of the natural world.)

There is no doubt that the argument of my book can be reinforced by elaboration on Nikolai Fyodorov's philosophical stand, revealed in his book *Philosophy of the Common Cause*. I have decided to designate this chapter to the referenced part of Fyodorov's philosophy. I also consider this chapter to be my tribute to this courageous and open-minded man, who started a new way of thinking about the human role in the universe.

Plato from "The School of Athens" by Raphael

In *Philosophy of the Common Cause,* Fyodorov calls for a common effort from humanity to conquer death and win immortality for all. His call was the start of the quest to revive the dead. Fyodorov believed that the struggle against death can and should become the most natural cause uniting all people on Earth, regardless of their nationality, race, citizenship, or wealth. He believed that mortality should stimulate humanity's common effort. His book touched on important issues of methodology and ethics of immortality and revitalization. He also saw mortality as evil, responsible for all human tragedies and misery.

Not knowing about today's need for an inspiring idea of the future, Fyodorov declared the achievement of immortality and revival as the greatest goal of society, especially science. The idea of immortality and revival of the dead, according to him, should become the subject of a comprehensive scientific inquiry.

Fyodorov was critical that death had been seen by scientists and, especially, philosophers as "inevitable, unconditional, and necessary." He called this a faulty methodology, which also results in infertility in the fight against death. The tenure of death, in his words, is a philosophical superstition that scientists view as they are moving on the imperfect road of the inductive method. Where scientists observe the death of successive generations of humankind, they come to the conclusion that death is an undeniable law. Philosophers, he said, have long inquired, "Why is life?" However, according to Fyodorov, more appropriate as defining the current human condition is the question, "Why is it that lives are suffering and dying and the dead are not animated?"

Fyodorov repeatedly said that only general scientific studies of aging, death, and the after-death condition could reveal the means to overcome death and transform human immortal life. In his words, all the findings relating to our universe, our planet, and our life are meaningless if we cannot use them to build our future.

To encourage the quest for immortality with the revival of the dead, Fyodorov explained that the revival of people who lived during the past is not a re-creation of their past physical form because it was imperfect, parasitic, centered on mortal existence. His call is to transform it into a self-creating, mind-controlled form, capable of infinite renewal.

Fyodorov believed that death is primarily a phenomenon still unknown; however, it does not mean that one cannot investigate it, understand it, and most importantly, reverse it. He calls death a blind force of nature that should be fought with and never surrendered to.

Fyodorov argued that the evolutionary process was directed toward increased intelligence and its role in the development of life. Man is the culmination of evolution, as well as its creator and director. He must direct it where his reasoning and morality dictate.

An interesting part of Fyodorov's philosophy is his relationship to nature and the Christian faith. He considered the cosmos to be a power without mind, and humans, a temporary mind without power. He suggested that man has a special role in the universe as a factor connecting God and nature. He believed that man is chosen by God to carry out his will. He saw the human conquest of death as part of God's will. He called mortality "a problem, which turns human ideals to a parody, a scandal to human intellect and a call to the Christian faith."

Obviously, Fyodorov would like to engage all of society in the battle for immortality. He held that human knowledge should never be hidden but must leave the laboratories and become the common property of all. According to Fyodorov, everyone must be learning and everything should be subjected to knowledge and certain action.

This will end my impression of Fyodorov's philosophy. Readers might notice that he discussed his belief in our total conquest of death without referring to life-death-revival cycles. Again, from my point of view, such cycles are unavoidable and necessary to keep eternal life meaningful. Nevertheless, despite the differences, I consider Nikolai Fyodorov to be my philosophical mentor.

CHAPTER VI

God or Nature?

On several occasions, I reminded readers that this book is about a concept of immortality achievable within the physical law.

It would not be my intention in this book to promote an atheistic philosophy. I advise philosophical neutrality about the origination of anything in any futuristic ideas.

Nevertheless, let's remember that in 1519, Hernán Cortés and six hundred of his Spanish soldiers easily conquered a large part of today's Mexico because invading Spaniards were believed to be gods. Let's keep in mind that the difference between the two civilizations did not exceed two or three centuries. Therefore, my constant thought is, who will be human in the very, very far future?

As stated many times in the past, nobody can prove (or disprove) the existence of God. Yes, I strongly promote the quest for immortality with the ability to revive the dead, because it is fair and it offers a healthy, motivating guideline for all people of goodwill.

However, any promotion of the origination philosophy would be against my principle to not take sides in the fruitless disputes of what or who governs the universe.

From the top left: Mat of ancient Egypt ritual, source; Wikipedia Commons; Symbol of Tao, Image of Buddha, Statue of Zeus in Olympia, source; Wikimedia; Fragment of Sisteen Chapel ceiling, Michael Angelo; Symbol of atom. The shown images represent only part of all known philosophies and beliefs.

Too many people died because of the discourse; to me, it leads only to a waste of society's energy. As long as a faith is harmless to others, we should leave the choice to personal feelings or needs.

There are too many unknowns. We have infinite possibilities about the origins and the future of the universe. There are many ideas about God, even within one religion. There are religions and beliefs whose sense has changed over time and place. For instance, in the Roman Empire, Christians were accused of being atheists and were prosecuted for not worshipping the Roman gods. There seems to be a growing number of those who believe that God may be acting within the natural law (for example, the Vatican approval of the theory of evolution). Nikolai Fyodorov believed that a man's collective action is an instrument of God's will.

Surprisingly, even atheistic groups are not monolithic; some appear to have their own subgroups. There are "Christian atheists" who do not believe in God but recognize Christian theological-philosophical moral thoughts developed by Jesus. There are atheists who believe in the existence of a force unknown to physics, but they are reluctant to name it or see in it a transcendental character. Finally, there is a quite influential group called "reductionists" (atheists-reductionists). The description of their philosophy of existence may be shortened to two sentences: Life never had any purpose and never will. The whole universe came from nothing and, in a distant future, will totally evaporate to nothing, not a speck of dust, no sigh, just total oblivion. For a long time, those reductionists have fought vigorously against less dismal visions of the future. Luckily, in recent years, their vision seems to be fading away.

What upsets me is that some theists and atheists proclaim the end of the world as inevitable no matter what is done from now on. Such a message definitely adds no "wings" to change people's attitude about the future of our planet. Nobody can possibly benefit from such calls, and none of the calls is provable until a certain event occurs. As a concerned humanist, I see the end-of-the-world theories as playing a demotivating role in the present struggle to save our planet from becoming uninhabitable.

Of course, I am not in a hurry to applaud the theories that play such a clearly negative role in society's effort to save humanity's future. What is interesting is that those who embraced the described dismal philosophy express no reservation or remorse. I am not the only one who wonders about people who are so submissive (and often cheerful) about a philosophy that makes human existence such a farce. I do not know what could possibly drive people to embrace such a vision. However, I am certain that it has nothing to do with somebody's sense of reality, level of courage, or scientific integrity.

For a long time, I had a close friend, a scientist, who was a hard-core reductionist. From time to time, we would have a friendly argument about what is rational to think about reality and what is not. I have to admit that after each discussion, my friend's passionate advocacy of his dismal visions of the future puzzled me. Then one day, he told me a life story, which I believe may contain the answer to his behavior.

According to the story, my friend was driving on the way to a vacation spot with his wife and two small kids. At some point of their travel, a car from the opposite side crossed the center lane and forced my friend off the road to avoid a head-on collision. My friend's car flipped over, landing on the roof. According to him, he and his family lost consciousness for a short time. Here, my friend ended his story with the following words: "After regaining consciousness, my first thought was, am I on the other side of the world?" There was silence between us when he added (with a little embarrassment in his voice), "Imagine with my beliefs having such a thought ... I found it funny."

My friend unintentionally revealed perhaps the true nature of his feelings. I think that it is rational to believe that almost all people have some strategies to cope with the prospect of death. One could feel that my friend did not think about death as something real or worth discussing. He seemed to expect that no matter how bad the future may be, there would be something positive for him. I think that many reductionists may use the strategy of keeping the death issue at bay (as nonexistent). This strategy apparently works for reductionists; however, most people cannot comprehend such an approach to their future. My main concern is that the message that reductionists promote has negative effects on people's attitude toward the future.

Of course, there are some troubling questions for theists too. An alleged "intelligent design" connected with the traditional beliefs may be seen as an excuse for many to do nothing to maintain our planet as habitable for the next generations. Besides, how do those believers justify the assumption that our planet is the only one that harbors life? According to astronomers, there are trillions of other planets in the universe, so why would Earth be such an exception? As an architect, I can assure anyone that no intelligent design would leave so much wasted space.

In conclusion, I declare no winners in the long-lasting debate of what or who is the source and driving force of the universe. My advice is to leave those questions to personal feelings and needs. Let's save our energy to do our part in securing conditions for the survival of future generations. From this point of view, I consider embracing immortality through revival of the dead as our best chance to succeed. This idea does not violate any law of physics, and it is still open to reasonable spiritual interpretations.

PART 2

CHAPTER VII

Humanism of a New Era

My spiritual mentor, Nikolai Fyodorov, argued that the struggle against death could become the most natural cause uniting all people of Earth, regardless of their nationality, race, citizenship, or wealth (he called this the Common Cause). This is exactly what I see as the duty of all people (and especially those who call themselves humanists or transhumanists). I cannot think of any more noble cause to pursue than working on the survival of our species, with the final goal to reach the ability to revive the dead. At minimum, the door to such an idea should remain always open.

Though it may be controversial for some, I must include globalization as a value helping to achieve the goal of immortality. Globalization unites people living in different parts of the planet, helping with prosperity, worldwide progress in science and technology, and popularization of humanistic ideas. Globalization helps more ideas and inventions reach more people in a shorter time. Globalization makes nuclear conflict less likely because it makes all nations depend on each other and understand each other.

I am aware that society is divided in regard to attitudes toward progress. Many see the idea of progress as nothing more than human lust for more possessions. Progress is blamed for many social problems, including the damage that is being done to our planet's ecology and the imperialistic behavior of some big countries. My opinion is different.

Why see progress as more evil than good?

There may be some problems with globalization, but there are many benefits that nobody wants to give up. The critics of progress need to look around and see how many modern devices they've taken for granted. Globalization helps us to make technological progress, and it should be obvious to everybody that advanced technologies may save us from many problems, especially the ones coming from the cosmos. Some of the cosmos challenges need to be explained.

Artistic rendering of a space rock crushing into Earth
Credit: Don Davis, NASA.

Astronomers claim to have catalogued most asteroids that are big enough to cause global destruction. They know their tracks and can predict their paths fairly well; they can also calculate where they will be at a given time. If they discovered an asteroid targeting Earth, scientists could redirect the object by using explosives or solar winds to deflect its course. However, our readiness to meet such challenges is not good enough.

Unfortunately, there are bigger challenges from the cosmos than the possibility of a collision with an asteroid or comet. According to astronomers, humanity will have to deal with the expiration of our sun, predicted to happen about five billion years from now. The problems with the sun are expected to occur much later than a collision with a large asteroid, but the solar threat would require extraordinary means to save humanity from extinction. So far, the sun's expiration is the most certain and serious challenge to humanity's survival. As we are told, if our planet stays in the same orbit as today, within one or two billion years, the swelling sun would wipe our planet clean of life.

The good news is that a group of scientists already has some plans to shift our planet away from the sun. It is theorized that a certain-sized asteroid could possibly be the solution by utilizing its gravitational pull to drag the Earth away from the sun. It is expected that dozens of asteroid passes could extend livable conditions on our planet for another two billion years. The increase of human technical ability within such time may be enough to save the planet.

Unfortunately, there are other giant events threatening the future of our planet. Our naked eyes see only a deceptive calm of a starry night. In reality, the universe is a forceful place. Births and deaths of stars, collisions of galaxies—all of these events eventually will affect our planet. Not long after our sun's demise, the neighboring Andromeda galaxy is supposed to merge with our own Milky Way galaxy. If this is not enough, astronomers warn of the possibility of a deadly gamma-ray burst from the nearest binary star system. They believe that about 450 million years ago, there was a mass extinction of life on our planet caused by such an event.

Is it still rational to expect that humanity would survive all the threats?

My answer is yes, and I am in good company. Here is a quote from the renowned British cosmologist Freeman Dyson: "We could break open a closed universe and change the topology of space-time so that only a part of it would collapse and another part of it would expand forever."*

What this respected scientist expects is that our descendants will have the titanic ability to alter the universe by controlling movements of planets, stars, and galaxies. Freeman Dyson is one of the distinguished scientists who challenge the official version of the "inevitable" end of the universe.

Another example is the already mentioned American cosmologist Frank Tipler. In his book *Physics of Immortality: God and Resurrection of the Dead*, he expects future civilization to control the final collapse of the universe (some decades ago, the "universe collapse" was a contemplated version

---

* "Time without End: Physics and Biology in an Open Universe," *Reviews of Modern Physics*, Vol. 51, No. 3, July 1979.

of the big bang theory). I guess the concept of an asteroid employed to move our planet away from the sun may be a miniature example of how extremely advanced civilization may deal with the need to move large celestial objects. In any case, my point is that the ideas of altering the universe seem to me more challenging than the task of reviving the dead.

Many seem to believe that colonization of the universe would dramatically increase humanity's chance to survive, at least as a species. As for now, we should brainstorm ideas to populate other parts of the universe sooner than later. As it was pointed out, we are sitting ducks living only on this planet.

The ability of humanity to survive depends on the conditions of our planet and the availability of technologies that can save humanity from danger.

The condition of our planet is a matter of human collective wisdom. The availability of technologies when they are needed is a matter of certain priorities and the pace of technological progress. With wisdom and sufficient technology always available ahead of a challenge, humanity could last an eternity.

For a very long time, philosophers have thought about a golden rule for moral behavior. The most popular golden rule of morality became "Do not do to others what you would not have done to you" (one can create the positive form of this rule by taking out the negation word, "not"). From this perspective, making an effort to leave better conditions for future generations to survive perfectly matches the golden rule. Please note that all criminal and immoral acts work against humanity's chance for survival. A murder of an innocent man deprives society of certain resources the deceased could provide. I have in mind the skills the murdered person could use for their family and society. The murder also costs time and resources of the police force and judicial system. On the contrary, friendly relationships between people increase society's capacity in all directions. We may say that all individual actions helping humanity's survival are signs of individual virtue. The golden rule may be based on our contribution to the goal of survival. Such judgment may help in cases when it is difficult to say whether a certain act is morally right or wrong.

In my conclusion, the quest for immortality through revival of the dead, also known as philosophy of the Common Cause, should become a leading goal for the humanism of the new era.

CHAPTER VIII

Dubious Alternative

*D*o we have any rational alternative to the immortality-through-revival-of-the-dead idea as humanity's long-run guideline for the future? My answer is no. In addition, we have to make the right choice rather quickly before it is too late to save humanity from extinction.

The closest competitor to the immortality-through-revival-of-the-dead idea is the proposal described earlier: biological immortality. As I already stated, this proposal seems to be too limited and too selective to meet the right goals. Just as a reminder, biological immortality is immunity from death caused by age or disease. People would continue to die in traumatic events like accidents, wars, or criminal acts. If nothing comes to revive people from traumatic deaths, biological immortality problems may outweigh its benefits. Here is why:

First, per today's statistics, an average member of biologically immortal society would have a chance to live no more than fourteen hundred years before meeting a traumatic death. The fear or anxiety to accidentally suffer a loss of life in a biologically immortal society would be much greater than it is today. Such loss would be seen as a lost chance to live forever. The psychological stress could take away all the good feeling about living much longer than now. People might be reluctant to work in hazardous jobs such as police, fire, or military positions. Some people may hesitate to go outside of their houses.

Second, there will be a risk of a permanent power grab by an oppressive regime. It may be a military coup or civilian fanatics taking over under the typical pretense of saving the nation from alleged political or economical chaos. In the past, many totalitarian systems, if they did not collapse, eased their oppressive rules due to pressure from society to bring democracy. It was most likely because when members of a junta got older, they were losing steam to continue their oppressive approach. In addition, by getting older, they perhaps become increasingly worried about an upcoming higher justice. However, in an era of biological immortality, it may be different. Biological immortality will keep the regime constantly young, energetic, and determined to stay in power forever. The worst, however, may be the corruptive power of those who have access to immortality procedures. Biological immortality may be quite costly and used only as a reward for loyalty to the oppressive government. With such a card in hand, even a very unpopular regime could stay in power forever. At best, we may expect serious abuses of power over the society with massive social tensions, leading to violence and disruption of life.

We may only hope that biological immortality would come in a time of substantially improved techniques to repair and resuscitate severely damaged bodies. Perhaps we live in a historical time of a breakthrough in dramatic extension of today's life span. It is possible that both biological immortality and the ability to resuscitate or resurrect life are not very far in time from predictions made by Aubrey de Grey and Raymond Kurzweil. The constant and gradual growth of our ability makes us often unaware that the future is today. We can expect that one day, the words *resuscitation* and *resurrection* will blend their meaning.

What about cryonics or life extensionism? Cryonics is a procedure used when people with terminal illness decide to preserve their body in a low-temperature container, hoping to be revived and have their disease cured by future technology. Cryonicists hope that through advanced science and technology, they will become biologically immortal. Unfortunately, cryonicists freeze not only their bodies but also valuable resources, which could be used to improve humanity's chance for surviving challenges. They may miscalculate their chances. Specially preserved bodies may be the easiest to resurrect; however, the future society may decide to put cryonicists at the end of the revival list, seeing them as selfish individuals.

Nevertheless, biological immortality and dramatic life extension may still be considered motivating factors in humanity's cause to survive as a species. We cannot say the same about the prophecies or theories predicting the end of the world. It does not matter where such predictions come from or in what time frame the end of the world is supposed to happen. My appeal to all the doomsday prophets is to restrain from anything that may undermine humanity's will to work for the future. Humanity's chances to overcome challenges depend on it.

Can't we just wait to see what the future will bring without making a guess as to what will happen to us? An old Roman proverb advises, *"Tempus omnia revilat"* ("Time reveals all truth"). This is not good advice either. Regarding the question of our fate, we cannot just sit tight and wait. One example of this case was the famous Manhattan Project, an American research and development program that produced the first atomic bomb in World War II.

At first, the idea of a nuclear bomb was only theoretical; nobody knew the outcome of research in such a direction. The decision to research the production of a bomb was very risky. Nobody knew how much money and time it would cost. Nobody knew what the end result of this research would be. Misconceptions about the power of the atomic bomb were big. After some heavy aerial bombing of Nazi Germany, their scientists tested for radiation in the largest bomb craters, suspecting that the atomic bomb was already in use.

Nevertheless, the US government decided that it could not risk losing the nuclear race to our adversaries. If Hitler were to win the race to get the bomb, it would be a nightmare for the free world. There were rumors that German scientists were close to constructing the bomb (in reality, they were substantially behind the United States, and Germany surrendered long before the bomb could be used). As it is known, the United States used two A-bombs, one on Hiroshima and another on Nagasaki, to win the war and save the lives of thousands of American soldiers.

The authors of the Manhattan Project made the right choice, and it was true that the Allies could not lose the race to create the first atomic bomb to Nazi Germany or Japan. A miscalculation in this matter would not be reversible.

In case of society being not serious about the long future of humanity, the stakes are even higher in a sense that it may be the only chance for each of us to survive our own death. Something like "to be or not to be" for humanity.

If we let ourselves become extinct and disappear into total oblivion while having a chance to reach a quite attractive future, it would make human history a pitiful farce. Falling into obscurity may not feel like a "dreamless sleep." Extinction may approach us as quite painful and scary, whether it is caused by environmental breakdown, nuclear war, or a collision with a large cosmic object.

In conclusion, there is no alternative but to keep the quest for immortality through revival of the dead alive at all times.

CHAPTER IX

Signs

*T*he main elements supporting the immortality-via-revival-of-the-dead idea are described in chapters I through IV. Moreover, I hope that the presented arguments were strong enough to convince readers that the idea is realistic. However, there are plenty of other signs that support this bold idea.

Please note that the most often repeated words associated with the signs are preservation, recovery, reconstruction, restoration, resuscitation, revival, or uncovering of something that existed in the past. All of them point in the same direction.

Uncovering the past may be an indication of a scientific curiosity. However, I believe that humanity's long and diligent efforts in this direction indicate something more than just professional passion. Many archaeologists, evolutionary biogeologists, and historians work long days to get tiny pieces of materials. Why do we need to spend tremendous time and money to say that we evolved from a microbe or that an ancient building looked a certain way? Of course, we do such things because this is what humanity is all about.

At the beginning of this book, I described how old buildings in Warsaw were looked upon as irreplaceable pieces of Polish national heritage. I am sure that the same has been felt in many civilized nations. The preservation and restoration of old buildings and sites commands a significant share of human activity today. And it is important to realize how much effort is sacrificed to truthfulness in reconstructing a historical monument.

In some cases, a monument damaged by an earthquake or war has been meticulously reconstructed, piece after piece. In other cases, many of its pieces (like columns, arches, cornices) are left on the ground, next to the main structure. Some may jump to the conclusion that lack of funds or negligence of some authorities causes the pieces to be left; however, they may be wrong.

Parthenon on the Athenian Acropolis, and renovation of one of its column, photo: Steve Swayne, for Wikimedia Commons

Quite often, the rules of monument conservation may require leaving the pieces where they lie. Most of the time, every piece of a monument must be restored true to its historical origin. Sometimes, putting back some elements of a monument is considered too much of a guess, violating conservation rules.

We may expect the same degree of truthfulness in biologists uncovering the truth of evolution.

As it was already mentioned in this book, diligence and curiosity go so far that scientists would like to resurrect a mammoth or early human. They want to study this long-extinct animal when it is alive. Some believe that resurrection of long-dead creatures could give scientists

Model of mammoth from Royal BC Museum in Victoria, author: Flying Puffin, source: Wikipedia Commons

the best idea about the nature of life. Japanese researchers believe that people could accomplish the task of resurrection within five years, thanks to recent advances in cloning technology. Their plan is to collect mammoth tissue from a carcass that was frozen in the Siberian permafrost.

Their hope is to recover an undamaged nucleus of a mammoth cell from this tissue and insert it into an elephant egg cell, from which the nucleus has been removed. This should create an embryo with mammoth genes.

Homo neanderthalensis head, reconstruction: John Gurche; photo: Tim Evanson, source: Wikipedia Commons

And this is not all; as I already mentioned, scientists contemplated resuscitating a Neanderthal, extinct about thirty thousand years ago. This controversial idea meets vigorous criticism because of strong ethical issues. The point is that a Neanderthal, with its low intellectual qualities, would be neither a human nor an ape. Of course, such resurrection may be risky for now. However, future science should be able to equalize the differences enough to make a Neanderthal's adaptation possible.

There are many other signs that indicate mysterious connections between the past, present, and future. How do you explain people who make special costly arrangements for the shipment of loved ones who died overseas? How do you explain the meticulous marking of graves and people spending hours conversing with someone who passed away?

A different type of indication, pointing in the direction of our destiny, I see is the relentless increase in the level of human control over nature.

Technological progress seems to accelerate. Each year, computer manufacturers offer products with higher processing speeds and increased memory. In addition, nanomedicine is just around the corner, ready to show its potential.

The electronic World Wide Web became the most powerful force for progress in knowledge, technology, economic growth, and even democratization. Ideas, discoveries, inventions, and technologies are rapidly shared with all people on the globe. The quick sharing of knowledge and experience powered up civilizations in places like Egypt and Rome. Life in those countries was concentrated in a few places; towns like Thebes and Memphis in Egypt or Rome had a high concentration of people. The concentration of people in those towns played a role similar to what the internet web plays today. The residents were acquainted with solutions, technologies, and ideas much faster than people who lived in the vast, mostly empty countryside. People living in big towns could see tools and techniques others used on a daily basis. They could copy and improve them for their own use. Finally, people could see how others organized communities and dealt with social problems.

CHAPTER X

Criticism and Answers

*S*o far, all immortality ideas, whether claimed to be achievable within or without natural law, met substantial criticism. What is surprising to me is that usually, highly hostile critics are also flawed in their criticism.

First, quite often critics do not even bother with defining what idea of immortality is on their minds: A religious one? Which religion? A secular one? Which concept?

Second, criticism of the immortality subject used to take two main forms: the objection that immortality could be achievable and the objection that immortality or eternal life would be desirable. Quite often, criticism overlaps the two strains, creating chaos in any argument.

Therefore, in my book, the main argument is divided into three distinct parts: *ability*, *desire*, and *sense*, giving critics a chance to address each part separately.

Third, there is a problem of many critics not doing their homework and thoroughly studying the subject of their criticism. Being unable to discover how certain problems could be resolved results in mistakes like the referenced comment that immortal life can't offer anything but an "eternal boredom." I believe that the vision of possible eternal life has been heavily distorted by cartoons of heaven in which people are dressed in white, suspended in an empty space, walking down heavenly alleys, singing songs, and otherwise doing nothing.

Of course, this would not excite an intelligent human being. Doing nothing? Excuse me! No new discoveries, no new structures, new poems, new pieces of art or music?

What a pitiful end to human history! Such a state of endless retirement with nothing to do may really be a torment for many. I can imagine the reaction from such giants of creativity as Leonardo da Vinci or Michelangelo, if they were revived and offered endless retirement.

I remember a story of Andrei Sakharov (1921–1989), the famous Russian nuclear physicist and laureate of the Nobel Peace Prize, being persecuted by the totalitarian Soviet regime.

Sakharov was an outspoken critic of the regime. The authorities tried to silence him in many ways. They put him in jail and refused to let anyone visit him, including his wife. Sakharov could not put his analytical mind to rest. He constantly needed to feed his brain with some form of analyses and calculations that he recorded in a small notebook. At some point, the regime decided to take away his notebook. Later, Sakharov admitted that it was a very painful psychological blow for him to have nothing to write on.

In the next chapter, I write extensively about the possible character of life in eternity because it is a very important aspect of immortality and the revival of the dead. Most people know very well what makes their lives meaningful. It is the time to accomplish something within that time. Time to learn and work, time to be entertained, time to relax. If we eliminate the factor of time, nothing would make sense, any meaningful activity would most likely die out, and intelligent society would probably change (mentally) into a colony of microbes. That is why I insist that the cycles of immortality, life-death-revival, are the only way of allowing individual souls and humanity as a group to enjoy meaningful life forever.

The fourth problem is the arrogance (or lack of imagination) of those who believe that they already know enough about physics to rule out some future achievements. Again, this is an example of a silly attempt to set limitations on higher entities by members of a more primitive civilization.

Throughout this book, I advocate for the idea of immortality and the revival of the dead being achievable through advanced knowledge and technology. A natural question would be, what does official science have to say about it? Here, I have to warn readers that official science will at best say nothing about such ideas. The natural reaction of science is to be suspicious of optimistic ideas, especially to be so close to the scenario proclaimed by some religions. Therefore, the positive claims receive much less attention than the negative ones. As a result, all ideas of immortality are left without scientific interest in them.

One may expect that the subject of immortality and revival of the dead may automatically raise many disreputable connotations as well.

Another problem is that many critics raise questions for which there are relatively easy answers (if somebody would bother to think about the answers). Here are some of the objections, followed by my short answers:

It has been argued that the quest for immortality is humanity's attempt to substitute themselves for God.

Answer: How would anyone know what God might want from us? Parents want their children to achieve the highest possible knowledge, position, and independence. If God were like our father, why would such an entity want us (his children) to remain limited, weak, and dependent on him throughout eternity?

There is a concern of cyborgization of humanity, dehumanization by infringement (of certain technology) in human biology.

Answer: Nobody is enthusiastic about having a body stuffed with technological devices to support

65

somebody's longevity; therefore, we may hope that medicine in the future will develop extensive methods to reproduce organic parts in a human body. However, so far, people often accept having technological body parts transplanted into their body to support their lives. Should we reject prosthetic limbs and artificial heart stimulators because there is too much technology in them? Or should we reject ear amplifiers, dental bridges, and eyeglasses? Of course, nobody wants to do that.

Overpopulation in the world caused by immortality is another problem raised during the debate.

Answer: Why is it a concern? It is hard to predict if immortal society will elect to have children or not. In any case, there are trillions of other planets awaiting colonization. So I wonder, what have those concerned been thinking about?

Some people raise the problem of early humans adapting to the new life, claiming it will consume tremendous amounts of time and resources.

Answer: Problem of time? Resources? The eternal societies will have plenty of time, won't they? And about the resources: Is it about money again?

I must stop at this point. All those questions seem to me never-ending (what is normal), and they are often trivial (what is abnormal). The rejection or criticism of the total immortality idea may only come from inconsistency, lazy thinking, prejudice, and what the famous British writer Arthur C. Clarke called "a failure of imagination." Below are Clarke's three laws, formulated to encourage society to think boldly about future achievements:

1. "When a distinguished but elderly scientist states that something is possible, he is almost certainly right. When he states that something is impossible, he is very probably wrong."
2. "The only way of discovering the limits of the possible is to venture a little way past them into the impossible."
3. "Any sufficiently advanced technology is indistinguishable from magic."

With those quotes of this intelligent man, I end my response to the criticism. Coming to an end of this book, I believe that the idea of immortality and revival of the dead would be incomplete without at least touching on some aspects of eternal life. In the next chapter, I offer my vision of it, hoping that it is what may interest our readers the most.

CHAPTER XI

Selected Issues of Eternity

Introduction

*T*he idea of a society living in a paradise-like environment is not new. Some readers may be familiar with the dreamland imagined in *Utopia,* a book written by Sir Thomas More, the sixteenth-century Renaissance humanist-idealist and counselor to Henry VIII of England.

Illustration for the 1518 edition of Utopia

I do not pretend to know about the mystical environment, commonly called "life after death," "another life," or "afterlife." However, I decided to address some aspects of immortal life, considering them to be an important part of the total immortality concept. Besides, somebody needs to counterbalance the images of afterlife planted in our subconsciousness by many humoristic cartoons or the silly "streets of gold" type of expectations.

As a result, even many religious people seem to have doubts about the existence of an afterlife. Therefore, I would like to present them with another point of view. There is a chance that today, collectively, we can establish better principles of an ideal society than those found in *Utopia*. In the sixteenth century, there was much less knowledge of the world than what we know today.

In this book, I have chosen the following aspects of eternal life: the environment, justice, work, and personal life. At the end of this chapter, I offer my opinion about the issue of extraterrestrial life.

Environment

The issue of the natural and man-made environment is placed at the top of this chapter for the following reason:

I found that providing an imaginary background of other issues might help make the unknown future world less strange. It is like putting a face on written information.

Also, through a large part of my professional life, I have been curious about how a future society might create an aesthetical match between the natural environment and constructed surroundings.

I refer to surroundings that provide the setting for human activity, ranging from the large-scale civic structures to personal shelters. I had fewer questions about the natural environment, assuming that the future society would impose higher environmental standards guaranteeing respect, care, and love for nature. One may safely bet that at some point of life, architects contemplated a list of what architecture would be like in the future. I tried very hard to imagine it and finally realized that in the extremely far future, architecture might lose its primary function, which is a shelter.

Creation of architectural space always involved the integration of intended form of life in the environment. However, in the era of total immortality, people may not need a shelter for personal use. Let's remind ourselves that a civilization having the ability to bring ancestors back to life should be able to control the natural world to a degree of high magic. This "magic" should include the ability to quickly build an object of any size and shape and undo the work, leaving almost no trace of it.

I expect that the members of the immortal society will be supplied with flexible personal womb-like enclosures, integrated with a person's body. These enclosures will be multifunctional and will provide protection from unwanted intrusions while offering perfect climatic conditions. Enclosures would allow for living or sleeping comfortably and safely anywhere on the ground (or suspended above the ground). Contrary to a knight's medieval armor, the enclosure would allow an instant physical contact between the surrounding world and other people. The described personal enclosure should provide maximum independence in any environment. Can one expect such an enclosure to ever be available? Again, the miracles of evolution support such an expectation. Interestingly, today's trend to make multifunctional, small electronic devices may signal the beginning of such a shelter. Also, I expect that no bridges or roads will be required for any practical purpose. (In my opinion, it is rational to expect fast and universal transportation above the ground.)

Despite the fantastic new technologies and the extreme independence of our descendants, the concepts of "home," "city," or "village" may be still valid for psychological reasons. In effect, the future eternal towns and villages may look similar to what we see today. Why?

First, let's recall the Warsaw experience, when the people's strong feeling about the past forced certain decisions of how reconstruction would take place. Therefore, I believe that many beautiful buildings will still be there in the new world. First, they may play a role of high-aesthetical-value landmarks, places of gathering, commemoration, or reflection like in the attached paintings (imaginary landscapes of ancient Greece) by Henri de Valenciennes:

Second, some public structures like museums, research labs, or sophisticated production equipment may still require architectural shelters. Such shelters may take any form, including some blended in landscape structures, as shown in the following illustration of Chapel in Rochamp designed by Le Corbusier.

Third, as the ancient masters of Greek design magnificently shaped the landscape, the eternal society may choose to continue their practice and impose on it certain structures of their own. It is an old call that humans should not submit passively to the environment but modify it to their own needs.

As this is the main theme of this book, humanity's existence in coherent and beautiful existential space will be a goal of the eternal society. It is my hope as an architect that nice pieces of architecture and other artistic creativity will always remain a part of human life.

Justice

The far future world of eternal life is totally unimaginable for most people. It is impossible to predict how issues in the future will be resolved with certainty. However, for fun we can take on this subject as well. This book

is based on an expectation that certain aspects of human nature will continue as long as humanity exists. Therefore, it should be the case with human desire to live in a world of justice and fairness.

These two qualities seem to be even more important than a life of comfort. What comes first to my mind about the issue of justice in eternity is an opportunity to be served retroactively.

It means that revived individuals may be judged for their entire past life. As we know, justice was not always served. Would it be possible to get enough documentation to judge all appropriately?

I believe that it is achievable, and the rest would be just a matter of setting right principles. To clarify this issue, we need to start by correcting once and for all a common mistake made by many about the nature of humanity: the habit of describing humanity as a negative entity. Here is a typical lament on humanity's alleged "evil" nature:

"The problem is our [humanity's] own individual egos working 'together' in disharmony. We need to cooperate in order to survive. But, we constantly bring pain on ourselves because we do everything we can to prosper at the expense of other people whenever we can. We care only for ourselves and no one else."

I did not mention the name of the author to save him embarrassment: Please note the use of "we" to stand for all of humanity, which should include the author of the quote (however, he would never admit to being as bad). Such statements seem to totally ignore the obvious diversity between mental characteristics (no wonder the prevailing vision of our future is so murky and negative).

Polish poet Czeslaw Milosz (a Nobel Laureate) calls such indiscriminate characterization a "sin of generalization." Unfortunately, this "sin" is quite common among many well-educated people. Perhaps the generalization is more entertaining; however, it should be clear that such indiscriminate statements about humanity are the mother of all evil, like bigotry, hate, wars, and atrocities. To make the problem worse, some psychologists made unproven claims that human behavior is totally curable and that the environment (meaning society) is guilty of the problem.

Frankly, I cannot tell whether bad behavior is curable or not. However, although mistakes are possible, the same bad people always do the bad acts, and the same good people remain good most of the time. Based on our own life, we can tell that rapid changes in behavior almost never happen. At this point, a natural question may be, whom should we call good and who is bad?

As described in chapter VII, there are some "golden" rules one can find in philosophical literature; apparently, none of them is perfect. For the purpose of my argument, let's consider a negative moral character somebody who wants to take from society more benefits than they are willing to give back. Unfortunately, nobody has done a study to reveal the ratio between good and bad characters, so in private discussion, it is even harder to find a consensus whether there are more good people than bad. Here, I am positive that the bad people do not outnumber the good.

If the bad people would prevail over the good, the present world would be in a state of a chaos. Anything created by the good would be undone, destroyed, or mismanaged by the bad. Acts of crime, vandalism, wars, or unrest would overwhelm society's ability to redo the damage. We would see constant acts of violence and criminals or henchmen of oppressive rulers roaming the streets. However, it is not the case.

Recent years have brought the spread of democracy to different parts of the world. Perhaps it is because globalization has educated people enough to awaken their taste for freedom. Perhaps good people learned how to deal with evil people or corrupt governments. We seem to be improving in civility and lawfulness in the world. Each year, new countries overthrow dictators and try to set some principles of democracy. Most countries belong to organizations that promote cooperation in preservation of peaceful coexistence, human rights, and even environment protection. Of course sometimes, perpetrators take over in some parts of the world, causing wars, destruction, and deaths of innocent people. However, despite new wars, acts of violence, and cases of injustice, humanist principles seem to be observed today more than ever. Those who have doubts should learn about the atrocities commonly tolerated and sanctioned throughout ancient and medieval times.

According to historians, in the first century BCE, after the Roman army defeated Spartacus's slave uprising, thousands of his fellow soldiers (former slaves) were crucified. One can imagine the terrible image of all the crosses being placed along the Appian Way from Capua to Rome.

If this is not enough, here are images depicting treatment of human beings by the "justice" system of the Middle Ages. I believe that the scenes do not need comments, except that this kind of justice was preserved often for poor, petty criminals, including those accused of witchcraft or heresy.

In all countries, secular and religious authorities commonly sanctioned the most cruel type of torture and public execution.

Today, state-sanctioned torture and public executions are very rare. Any atrocities committed by governments or known groups are instantly condemned by the entire world. Even acts of brutality or cruelty by individuals find worldwide outrage and condemnation. The question arises, are we better today? Is the better part of society now holding the bad people responsible for their acts? I believe that the right answer is in the second assumption. Now we have more democracies in the world than ever. It means that today, there are better chances for good people to stay in power who will set the appropriate rules.

Some may question such an opinion, pointing at the crime and violence in the daily news. However, we have to keep in mind why that is so: Today, we have more people than ever in the past. For instance, the first census in 1801 revealed that the population of

Great Britain was only 10.5 million. As we know, that is less than many big cities throughout the world today. Another reason is that fewer people can do more damage in less time than ever. A single maniac with an assault rifle and large magazine can kill dozens of people in a minute. A few terrorists can deploy weapons of mass destruction and kill tens of thousands instantly. In addition, the media usually picks the most shocking or horrific stories.

All together, advanced technology and globalization of the news makes it appear that violence and incivility and injustice are growing worse. There should be no doubt that we have made progress in crime prevention, criminal investigations, understanding of behavioral problems, forensic science, and improved surveillance systems.

There are indications that we are making progress in reaching more civility than ever in the past. As for the future, it is rational to expect that in the universal immortality era, criminals will be under much higher control than today.

Now, let's go back to the question of retroactive justice. Assuming that the members of the eternal society enjoy exceptionally good justice, here is a question: Should bad individuals be brought to new life and face the "final justice," or should they be left dead in graves?

I guess that the first common reaction to such a question would be, "Keep the bad guys dead in graves and make sure they will never rise." However, this would not be the best answer. If such a call were followed, justice would be severely compromised.

As we know, there may be different levels of being good or bad. Leaving those in their graves whom we might call bad would violate the proportionality of punishment to crime. Such proportionality is a basic principle of justice. In *Utopia,* Thomas More criticized his fellow citizens for hanging murderers as well as those who stole a chicken. Though it was a common thing in medieval times to die of hunger, being hanged for stealing a chicken seems a very cruel and disproportional punishment. Even a petty criminal who unintentionally kills during a robbery may not be as evil as other monsters known from history (e.g., Hitler, Stalin, Caligula, Pol Pot, or Vlad the Impaler). The justice would be far from being perfect if petty criminals were left in graves sharing the fate as the most evil people ever known.

However, looking at the case further: Is it rational to expect that the future intelligent society will resurrect the human monsters just to make them suffer endless physical torments (like in the biblical hell)? Frankly, I doubt that any sophisticated society now or in the future would apply such punishment. So how could the civility and the proportionality of crime and punishment work together?

As of now, nobody can tell for certain what is the main cause of bad behavior and whether it is curable at all. If bad behavior is curable, then we will have a set of unknown philosophical issues, about which I do not have any answers. However, we cannot rule out a possibility that a substantial number of evil people will always remain a part of what we call humanity. If this is the case, I see one universal rule to resolve the problem of the final justice for all:

It is based on the assumption that all who commit bad acts will have their mentality studied and evaluated to the most accurate degree. It is quite possible that the far future society will be able to identify all bad characters and identify precisely the level of their mentality. The ideal justice could be served when people of a certain level of mentality were separated with no free contact with people possessing higher mental character. Of course, in practice it would be more complicated, since even within one family, there are different levels of mental characters. Nevertheless, the general principle of separation of bad and good (if practically possible) may be the essence of the future system of justice for all, including the revived people from the past.

It is easy to imagine that life in a group consisting of the worst mental characters would be a physical and mental torment. This group would not be able to make or preserve anything to make their life easy. They would constantly struggle to survive, to get food or water, or to build a shelter. They would live within the rule of the jungle; however, they would have a much higher sense of what they are than animals. They would live day and night in constant fear of being mugged, tortured, or killed by other evil humans. There would be no predators or victims but predators and victims in one. This group's life would be a living hell, marked by many cases of violent deaths and suicides of those who would rather die than continue to live this way. The only question is, what ought the governing society do? Should they revive the dead criminals repeatedly to a new ordeal, or finally leave them dead?

By high contrast, I want to outline the possible life of a group consisting of the best mental characters:

This group would have a chance to enjoy peace and harmony, where relationships with others would always be friendly and full of compassion. The best moral characters would decide about the fairness and justice at work and other public life. Everybody would be ready to help in case of any trouble. There would be no need for police or security guards of any sort, no need for locks, fences, or security barriers. There would be no fear of intruders or concern about protecting personal belongings. Both urbanized and secluded places would be safe, day and night.

Residents of this environment would be free from the stresses we endure in our daily lives. Their long life span would be supported by technology to revive unfortunate individuals. All of these benefits should have them feel like living in a paradise.

Is the described arrangement possible? It is hard to say; it may be difficult because the majority of individuals would fall into a category between the worst and the best. The described model of life for the two separated groups, representing two extremely opposite mental characters, may sound Orwellian. However, separation along the mental character line (if possible) seems to be the best way to satisfy justice and civility. Finally, one can always ask, what is the better option?

I am aware that I did not address all aspects of justice and fairness. For instance, how can we preserve contact within the closest family members, representing different levels of moral characters? What about marriage between partners of two different moral characters? Again, we do not know enough about human nature. However, as in the other parts of eternal life, we can expect that in the immortal future, justice and fairness will be much higher than they are today.

Work

Work is a place that many of us see as very imperfect in regard to the relationships among the systems of production, wages, promotions, and so on. Therefore, justice and fairness must be extended to such places for two reasons. One is the human factor, and the other is that justice at work improves effectiveness. Of course, proposed regulations should restrain employers from overregulation, which might stifle an enterprise's need for flexibility.

We may expect excellent work conditions and pleasant humanistic relationships in the workplace to be the norm in future workplaces. There is a lot to do in this field for psychologists, as there is no reason why a laborer's occupation should not be as entertaining as a football game. And I have in mind occupations not necessarily as deadly as North Sea crab fishing, ice-road trucking, or cutting heavy timber. I think about just presentations of ways jobs are performed, such as the "finest marvels of technology" or "how the stuff works."

Even today, visual entertainment seems to be shifting toward nonfiction programs. We may expect that future occupations, especially exploration of other parts of the universe or uncovering the past, will deliver lots of excitement. Some sophisticated audiovisual techniques should make presentations of these occupations very attractive to watch.

Personal Life

As I have already mentioned, there are some strong indications that in the long run, humanity as a whole will attain extraordinary power and knowledge.

This, I hope, should ease any skepticism about things that I expect to happen in the future. Our far future descendants should control the quantum world enough to change people's body size and shape, similar to how we dress today. Different sizes for some personal contacts, different ones for work, different ones for space travel. The latest application could be useful for a spaceship crew being able to shrink their body size to decrease food and water consumption during long interstellar travel.

The ability to dramatically change somebody's appearance explains why I believe it should not be a problem to assimilate past generations in the new eternal world. As I already mentioned, genetic engineering would equalize intellectual and mental assimilation. We can expect that the part of the universe within accessible range will represent a similar culture and appearance to now.

In the *Star Wars* movie saga, we see a dramatic variety of different creatures living together. However, I believe that even a very sophisticated civilization may feel uneasy to have some strange-looking (and -thinking) creatures around them.

A little more sophisticated issue is that most people would like to look attractive all the time to attract a certain partner. Most men and women would choose to be in the age range of twenty to twenty-two, so they would have a similarity in appearance. Of course, different people may prefer a somewhat different type of appearance.

There may be other ways to differentiate between people. It could be important in the case of members of the same family. Some critics lament that grandparents will be the same age as (and now look similar to) their grandchildren, but why would it pose such a problem? There may be a thousand ways to identify a person. Future scientists may create in each person special feelings about the family members that we feel today. Isn't it correct that we see our fifty-year-old children as still children?

A person's physical appearance suggests character traits regardless of whether that person in fact possesses those traits. In new life, what will really count as a personal value will be one's mental character. This may have a profound effect, especially on choosing a partner for a long-lasting romantic relationship. I will elaborate a little more on this subject.

Things that make our life worth living may be different for different ages and different people. For some it may be art, for others music, science, or something else.

When we were young, the things that made us happy were as simple as the words in the old song by Eden Ahbez, "Nature Boy." The song tells a fantasy of a "strange enchanted boy ... who wandered very far" only to learn that

> *The greatest thing*
> *You will ever learn*
> *Is just to love and*
> *Be loved in return.*

Those words tell all about this great feeling and how our happiness often depends on it.

I read one objectionist's complaint that a romantic relationship in eternity cannot be a happy one due to a lack of novelty. Well, I have words of advice for this "noveltist": in the new life, he may find himself in a dangerous human environment in which he will encounter only novelties and no moments of quiet.

Seriously, romantic love is a specific subject that's very difficult to discuss in objective terms. One can list a half dozen types of romantic love, and it is unlikely that two people would have experienced all of them in the same way. In chapter IV, I explained what should make an eternal life meaningful and happy. The indicated principle should work for any part of life, including romantic relationships.

Question of Extraterrestrial Life

Honestly, I do not understand why people are so excited about the possibility of extraterrestrial contact. Is the excitement driven by a hope that they could resolve our problems and fulfill our dreams?

Many scientists suggest that some extraterrestrial civilizations may be millions of years older than ours. However, I would not count on help from anybody beyond our planet. Yes, advanced aliens might be peaceful and friendly to us, but it would be like friendship between wild animals and researchers studying them in their natural environment. The Manhattan Project story tells us that advanced technology must always pair with advancement of humanist principles. I believe that here humanity still has some work to do. We must pursue our goals gradually on our own.

Yes, it is very rational to expect that in such a vast universe there are many planets that harbor life. There is a strong expectation of traces of life even in our solar system, like Mars or Jupiter's moon Europa. However, the existence of intelligent extraterrestrial life is a different story.

Our planet seems to have exceptional tuning for life of a higher complexity. Besides such elements as climate and physical forces (like gravitation), all life on Earth is based upon some specific chemical elements existing in an exact size and proportion. There is a one to some billions chance of repeating exactly the same favorable conditions anywhere in the universe. Therefore, many astrobiologists believe that most extraterrestrial life is in microorganism form; it is probably very strange to us. It would be exciting to receive a "hello" from some extraterrestrial aliens today, but the decades-long surveys of the universe have so far come up empty-handed.

Also, there is this big problem of distances. In 1977, NASA's *Voyager 1* left for the stars, containing a golden plate on which was engraved information about humans. Traveling seventeen kilometers (10.56 miles) per second, this spacecraft needed thirty-five years to reach the edge of our solar system.

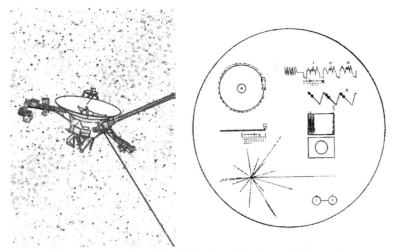

Voyager and gold-plated audiovisual disc, with information about humans. Linear form drawn by author based on original spacecraft images (credit: NASA)

Although the *Voyager 1* mission has little practical meaning, in my opinion it has a very high value of being inspirational to a cause like the one promoted in this book.

Nevertheless, it is still rational to expect that human exploration of the universe will eventually bring an encounter with some extraterrestrial civilizations. However, it is unlikely for us to physically meet an intelligent extraterrestrial life anytime soon. One thing I am certain is that civilizations of much higher development than ours will never try to kill all humans (like we often see in the movies).

There is a reason to expect that high technologies and high technical ability are products of higher civility and compassion. Somehow, the most developed countries are also technologically the most advanced. Therefore, I would expect a rather friendly visit than a violent one. The possible outcome of such contact is the subject of a separate book.

Sorry, but there are too many unknowns holding me from more elaboration on the extraterrestrial subject.

CHAPTER XII

Summary and Final Conclusion

*T*here is no way anybody can be certain about the individual or collective fate of humanity. Nobody can even guarantee our survival over the next century; however, as I repeat it over and over again, we may greatly improve our odds, and this is what this book is about.

The idea of immortality and revival of the dead passionately advocated by Nikolai Fyodorov, Hans Moravec, and Frank Tipler gives us the direction. Their inspirational work offers a chance for us to see the future in a different light. We must act as we are a part of the future one way or another; there is too much at stake to not act.

Skeptics may argue that the idea promoted in this book is a wishful fantasy versus their view of reality, which happens to be negative. But we are not giving up our intellectual integrity. In the past, deniers and skeptics of future human achievements quite often revealed a lack of imagination resulting in poor judgment. Each time, the deniers and skeptics thought that they had a perfect basis for their pessimistic opinions, which turned out to be incorrect.

Only a very long period of human development can reveal if the promoted idea is true or not. For now, the attractive goal to pursue the most universal immortality has at least the positive motivating value. As I already stated, today's society seems to need a strong motivation to save our planet for future generations. Thinking of myself as a humanist, I decided to leave for others the deliberation of how the immortality and revival of the dead could be technically possible. My role has been to check how the idea of immortality works with our human nature and how it may resolve societal problems and make us happy.

In the case of the idea that I promote in this book, all major parts of the claim seem to have a solid base in human nature, trends, and logic. As we can see, human *ability* is a function of time. The claim that our descendants should be able to revive the dead and achieve total immortality is supported by what we know about evolution. The transformation of a powerless microbe to a species like us proves that in our capacity there are no limits other than our *desire*.

I pointed at four factors, which would guarantee that our mighty descendants will have sufficient *desire* to revive all who ever lived (within a scope described in chapter III). The factors are as follows:

- social bonds
- human need for justice
- scientific curiosity
- growing civility and compassion

Finally, I demonstrated in this book that it is possible to make eternal existence happy and meaningful. Again, here are the rules:

In practice, immortality (within the natural law) must have a form of life-death-revival cycles because total immunity from death is impossible as long as we are humans. We are not perfect, and we will make mistakes that from time to time lead to somebody's death. The expected future ability to revive the dead will make people practically immortal. In addition, the uninterrupted life span on average will be extremely long and the time of being dead will shrink.

There is another necessity for the life-death-revival cycles; even a very remote prospect of being temporarily dead will preserve in people's minds the value of time (as it is now when we are mortal). People will never stop their progress in knowledge and technology due to this factor, which would improve the odds to survive and stay alive. The life-death-revival cycles will most likely remain forever as an inevitable part of the immortality philosophy.

Now I would like to describe how I see the path on which humanity has been walking from the time of the first life on our planet.

My instinct tells me that human complexity, level of ability, and the effort to improve whatever is of human interest will continue forever. Presented in the same page is a graphical representation of the path humanity most likely has been walking on.

In this graph, the curved line represents humanity's progress from the left to right. The curved line is in asymptotic relation to the vertical straight line, symbolizing omnipotence and omniscience.

In mathematics, an asymptotic relationship means that the curved line approaches the straight line but never meets it. Such endless separation of one line approaching another is possible when the curved line constantly unveils from the straight line. This is, in my opinion, the path on which humanity walks.

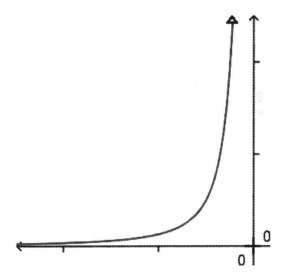

Who or what holds the vertical line, one may ask. The answer, again, is nobody knows and, perhaps, never will.

At the end, I would like to bring one more argument in support of the idea just presented in this book. Architects, like other artists, instill aesthetics and a sense of beauty in their work.

Moreover, quite often, mathematicians, physicists, or philosophers also use such terms as "elegant" or "beautiful" to describe a particularly creative discovery, theory, or equation.

Judging from this point of view, I see the idea of immortality and revival of the dead as being the most truthful and beautiful vision of the future.

In this book, I frequently mention humanist values or humanist principles. Many readers may be aware that those values and principles were established in 2002 in a declaration by the Humanist Movement in Amsterdam. This statement reveals the fundamental principles of modern humanism.

Following this, to be fair, I included the Transhumanist Declaration, which advocates bold and inspiring futurist ideas like the subject of this book. I don't see a reason to not adapt both declarations as one set of principles, guiding the lives of present and future generations.

Appendix 1 and appendix 2 contain copies of each movement's declaration.

APPENDIX 1

Humanist Amsterdam Declaration 2002

*H*umanism is the outcome of a long tradition of free thought that has inspired many of the world's great thinkers and creative artists and gave rise to science itself. The fundamentals of modern humanism are as follows:

1. Humanism is ethical. It affirms the worth, dignity, and autonomy of the individual and the right of every human being to the greatest possible freedom compatible with the rights of others. Humanists have a duty of care to all of humanity including future generations. Humanists believe that morality is an intrinsic part of human nature based on understanding and a concern for others, needing no external sanction.

2. Humanism is rational. It seeks to use science creatively, not destructively. Humanists believe that the solutions to the world's problems lie in human thoughts and actions rather than divine intervention. Humanism advocates the application of the methods of

science and free inquiry to the problems of human welfare, but humanists also believe that the application of science and technology must be tempered by human values. Science gives us the means but human values must propose the ends.

3. Humanism supports democracy and human rights. Humanism aims at the fullest possible development of every human being. It holds that democracy and human development are matters of right. The principles of democracy and human rights can be applied to many human relationships and are not restricted to methods of government.

4. Humanism insists that personal liberty must be combined with social responsibility. Humanism ventures to build a world on the idea of the free person responsible to society, and recognizes our dependence and responsibility for the natural world. Humanism is undogmatic, imposing no creed upon its adherents. It is thus committed to education free from indoctrination.

5. Humanism is a response to the widespread demand for an alternative belief to dogmatic religion. The world's major religions claim to be based on revelations fixed for all time, and many seek to impose their world-views on all of humanity. Humanism recognizes that reliable knowledge of the world and ourselves arises through a continuing process of observation, evaluation, and revision.

6. Humanism values artistic creativity and imagination and recognizes the transforming power of art. Humanism affirms the importance of literature, music, and the visual

and performing arts for personal development and fulfillment.

7. Humanism is a life stance aiming at the maximum possible fulfillment through the cultivation of ethical and creative living. It offers an ethical and rational means of addressing the challenges of our times. Humanism can be a way of life for everyone everywhere.

Our primary task is to make human beings aware in the simplest terms of what humanism can mean to them and what it commits them to do. By utilizing free inquiry, the power of science, and creative imagination for the furtherance of peace and in the service of compassion, we have confidence that we have the means to solve the problems that confront us all. We call upon all who share this conviction to associate themselves with us in this endeavor.

IHEU Congress 2002

APPENDIX 2

*Transhumanist Declaration**

1. Humanity stands to be profoundly affected by science and technology in the future. We envision the possibility of broadening human potential by overcoming aging, cognitive shortcomings, involuntary suffering, and our confinement to planet Earth.
2. We believe that humanity's potential is still mostly unrealized. There are possible scenarios that lead to wonderful and exceedingly worthwhile enhanced human conditions.
3. We recognize that humanity faces serious risks, especially from the misuse of new technologies. There are possible realistic

* The Transhumanist Declaration was originally crafted in 1998 by an international group of authors: Doug Baily, Anders Sandberg, Gustavo Alves, Max More, Holger Wagner, Natasha Vita-More, Eugene Leitl, Bernie Staring, David Pearce, Bill Fantegrossi, Dalibor van den Otter, Ralf Fletcher, Kathryn Aegis, Tom Morrow, Alexander Chislenko, Lee Daniel Crocker, Darren Reynolds, Keith Elis, Thom Quinn, Mikhail Sverdlov, Arjen Kamphuis, Shane Spaulding, and Nick Bostrom. This Transhumanist Declaration has been modified over the years by several authors and organizations. It was adopted by the Humanity+ Board in March 2009.

scenarios that lead to the loss of most, or even all, of what we hold valuable. Some of these scenarios are drastic, others are subtle. Although all progress is change, not all change is progress.

4. Research effort need to be invested into understanding these prospects. We need to carefully deliberate how best to reduce risks and expedite beneficial applications. We also need forums where people can constructively discuss what should be done, and a social order where responsible decisions can be implemented.

5. Reduction of existential risks, and development of means for the preservation of life and health, the alleviation of grave suffering, and the improvement of human foresight and wisdom should be pursued as urgent priorities, and heavily funded.

6. Policy making ought to be guided by responsible and inclusive moral vision, taking seriously both opportunities and risks, respecting autonomy and individual rights, and showing solidarity with and concern for the interests and dignity of all people around the globe. We must also consider our moral responsibilities towards generations that will exist in the future.

7. We advocate the well-being of all sentience, including humans, non-human animals, and any future artificial intellects, modified life forms, or other intelligences to which technological and scientific advance may give rise.

8. We favour allowing individuals wide personal choice over how they enable their lives. This includes use of techniques that may be developed to assist memory, concentration, and mental energy; life extension therapies; reproductive choice technologies; cryonics procedures; and many other possible human modification and enhancement technologies.

BIBLIOGRAPHY

Aczel, Amir. *Pendulum: Leon Foucault and the Triumph of Science.* Washington Square Press.

Baillie, John. *And the Life Everlasting.* Oxford University Press: London, 1956.

Dawkins, Richard. *The Biggest Show on Earth: The Evidence for Evolution.* Free Press, 2009.

Deutsch, David. *The Fabric of Reality.* Allen Lane, Penguin Press, 1997.

Dyson, Freeman. *Infinite in All Directions.* HarperCollins, 1998.

Fuller, Buckminster. *Operating Manual for Spaceship Earth.* Pocket Books, 1972.

Fuller, Buckminster. *Utopia or Oblivion.* Bantam Books, 1969.

Hawking, Stephen. *A Brief History of Time.* Bantam Dell Publishing Group, 1988.

International Humanist and Ethical Union. *Amsterdam Declaration 2002.*

Kurzweil, Raymond. *The Singularity Is Near.* New York: Viking 2005.

Law, Stephen. *The Great Philosophers.* Quercus Publishing, 2007.

Lewin, Roger. *Thread of Life.* Smithsonian Books, 1989.

Moravec, Hans. *Mind Children: The Future of Robot and Human Intelligence.* Harvard University Press, 1990.

More, Thomas. *Utopia.* Norton and Company, 1975.

Morrison, Philip, and Phylis Morrison. *The Ring of Truth.* Random House, 1987.

Murchie, Guy. *The Seven Mysteries of Life.* Houghton-Mifflin, 1978.

National Geographic Magazine. "Front Line of Discovery." National Geographic Society, 1995.

Norberg-Shultz, Christian. *Existence, Space & Architecture.* Praeger Publishers, 1971.

Sagan, Carl. *Cosmos.* Random House, 1980.

Stroll, Avrum. *Did My Genes Make Me Do It?* Oneworld Publications, 2004.

Tippler, Frank. *The Physics of Immortality: Modern Cosmology, God and the Resurrection of the Dead.* New York: Doubleday, 1994.

Żylina-Chudzik, Julia. *Activist Eschatology of Nikolai Fyodorov.* Graduate work, 1995.

Transhumanism (H+). *Transhumanist Declaration.*